THE
BREAKUP

The Breakup
© 2024 by Mag Gabbert

No part of this book may be used or reproduced in any manner whatsoever without written permission except in the case of brief quotations embodied in critical articles and reviews.

Design & Layout by Adam Deutsch
Cover Art is "Passive Aggressive" by Kelly Puissegur

ISBN: 978-1-943899-20-3

An edition of this collection was selected by Kaveh Akbar as winner of the 2022 Baltic Writers Residency Chapbook Award

THE
BREAKUP

MAG GABBERT

Table of Contents

[in the beginning] 1
[we visited drawings] 2
[throughout the whole winter] 3
[listening to stormy weather] 4
[my favorite shows] 5
[sometimes my brain] 6
[I stare out] 7
[the manicurist] 8
[I'm already] 9
[at a theater] 10
[sun bleaches] 11
[would he rather] 12
[lately I've been] 13
[why do I miss him] 14
[to finally change] 15
[can't stop thinking] 16
[another dismal night] 17
[I pluck] 18
[unfinished dinners] 19
[soon as I climb] 20
[it's like breathing] 21
[this migraine] 22

Acknowledgments 24
Note on the Form 25

```
in the beginning he tenderly kissed my forehead
          in                          my      head
i     beg                            for
                ten
        inning              s                 a
                    tender
                     end
```

```
we visited drawings of withered flowers at a museum
                           here        at a
                                  lower
        site               the                muse
        visited    i
        sit                with
                           her
                raw           red
                wings
```

```
throughout the whole winter, my heart switches directions
                                a              dire
           hole  in    my  ear
                  i        hear
  rough                            witches
           who                              direct
                       my       wit
                 win
```

```
listening to stormy weather has become sentimental
                        the                    time
                             has     come
            to
list           my                              men
                        a                      mental
             storm       he              sent
                             has become

   ten
```

```
my favorite shows seem so asinine and shallow now
                          as        a
        rite               i            allow
my favorite              sin
    or                   nine
                         in
              see
         how              i          hallow
     it                              all
```

```
sometimes my brain feels totally scrambled
so             in
        my bra          a      ram  led
    me                  to
            rain
             i                     ambled
               in  eels            bled
```

```
I stare out the windows of my apartment like a goldfish
                do                    men  like
                            art
                                                    is
                wind                            old
    a                       part
                    of          me                  is
                                        like a
    star        i                           go
          out
```

```
the manicurist paints my nails the color of pink seashells
the man        aint my                              hell
 he       is                            ink
    an                       ail     or   pin
      manic    pain                           ashe s
                in         the            sea
```

```
I'm already a too-comfortable beast with meat on my bones
I'm                                    at
         a           fort        with    a
                        table
                     for                             one
                  able beast
        ready  to                        eat
                     or     be   with me
```

```
at a theater with friends I stand alone and barely speak
            it    ends         on  a   bare   peak
                  friends              are
at   the                                bar
                   I                      rely
                              on
     heat
```

```
sun bleaches the vibrant colorful names off my books
                                            my
    aches
  each         rant              off
                    color
       the              name of my boo
              vibra t o  r
```

```
would he rather be mistaken than be together
would           i
        rather be mist      than        ether
        rather                          get
          the       stake than
            be       a
        rat                             he
would   rather      take                her
```

```
lately I've been too tired to bathe or shave my hairy skin
                too
late            to        bat
                          at              my
                    ire                                 kin
                to        a
          bee   i                   have
                    red                       hair   i
ate                           the             air
```

```
why do I miss him despite the fact that he was never nice to me
why        is        it         that                    ice
                     despite the                    eve
           is                              a
                     pit
why do I                        act                      nice
                                           as  ever
                     despite     that
                     spit
```

to finally change approaches, I gather up my shame
                              at
                              the
    final   hang   up
                         I   am
            an
        ally
to.   the
                    roaches
        all   up
        in   me

```
can't stop thinking about flying off to a swanky resort
can't  top         a
             king about           to         resort
      to                  lying
         in    a                            sort
                             of    swan    so
                          i
        thin      out
```

```
another dismal night spent holding a pillow
    the          night
          is
an                              old     pill
    he   is                 holding
  no      i m
  not                                    ill
```

```
I pluck lots of dandelion thistles to make an arrangement
                and                                arrange
        lots of                                        men
                      on this                          gem
            of   a    lion                             range
                                        to make
    luck           and
                   a  deli
```

```
unfinished dinners begin to soften in the fridge
                gin to soften    the ridge
                     to
               be                    rid
                        of     the
              inner
    fin  he                 often
      is     i
       shed
```

```
soon as I climb out of bed I want to slip beneath the covers again
soon    I                    want to        eat            again
                                                           gain
                                 lip                    s
                                 to slip                    in
                                               the cove
           climb out
   on                           a          neat
         limb
```

```
it's like breathing on a dim undiscovered planet
                                o       plan
                  on a
            thin
         breathing
            thing
              in      a       disco
                              disc
it's like              im       over
it
```

```
this migraine: a dense orchard full of iridescent parrots
              a            hard         ride
                      or   a                   descent
this          den
 is                                full of
his          dense                            scent
                                of              rot
```

Acknowledgments

I would like to thank the following journals for first publishing these sections of the poem, some of which now appear in revised forms:

Four Way Review: "[throughout the whole winter]," "[I'm already]"

Gigantic Sequins: "[I stare out]," "[the manicurist]," "[why do I miss him]"

Gulf Coast: "[sometimes my brain]"

New Delta Review: "[in the beginning]," "[at a theater]"

Seneca Review: "[sun bleaches]," "[another dismal night]," "[soon as I climb]"

Sugar House Review: "[we visited drawings]," "[would he rather]," "[unfinished dinners]," "[this migraine]"

The sections "[I stare out]" and "[the manicurist]" also appear in my full-length collection, SEX DEPRESSION ANIMALS (Mad Creek Books, 2023).

Thank you, Kaveh Akbar, who selected this little collection as the winner of the 2022 Baltic Writing Residencies Chapbook Prize.

Thank you, as well, to Kelly Puissegur for allowing me the use of your fabulous painting "Passive Aggressive" on the cover of this book, and to Adam Deutsch of Cooper Dillon Books for lending your design expertise. Finally, as always, thank you thank you to my "real" family and to my chosen family of poets and friends for your kindness and love and support of all of my projects, including this one. You all know who you are. I love you.

A Note On The Form
As you may have realized, each section of this poem was constructed using a specific kind of self-erasure. After conducting a bit of research and discussing the topic with colleagues and peers, I feel certain that it is a form I invented, so I'm calling this type of poem 'a breakup.'

The process of writing a breakup begins with just a single, short sentence. For example, "It's like breathing on a dim undiscovered planet." Then, that sentence must be copied and pasted a number of times below itself, until the page becomes a field of repeating lines. At that point, the challenge is to locate as many words as possible within the existing words of the first sentence, so that these new words might convey a new narrative—one that ideally comments upon, follows, or otherwise sheds light on the original line. Once your words are decided upon, any unnecessary letters beneath the initial sentence must finally be changed to white font, so that only the planned erasure remains visible.

I'll illustrate that process below using grey font and underlined text instead:

<u>**it's like breathing on a dim undiscovered planet**</u>
it's like breathing on a dim undiscovered <u>**plan**</u>et
it's like breathing <u>**on a**</u> dim undiscovered planet
it's like brea<u>**thing**</u> on a dim undiscovered planet
it's like <u>**breathing**</u> on a dim undiscovered planet
it's like brea<u>**thing**</u> on a dim undiscovered planet
it's like breath<u>**in**</u>g on <u>**a**</u> dim un<u>**disco**</u>vered planet
it's like breathing on a dim un<u>**disc**</u>overed planet
<u>**it's like**</u> breathing on a d<u>**im**</u> undisc<u>**over**</u>ed planet
<u>**it**</u>'s like breathing on a dim undiscovered planet

Now, I wish you the best of luck with crafting your own breakup poems!

                                                                                                       MG

Mag Gabbert is also the author of SEX DEPRESSION ANIMALS, which was selected by Kathy Fagan as the winner of the 2021 Charles B. Wheeler Prize in Poetry, and the chapbook *Minml Poems* (Cooper Dillon Books, 2020). She is the recipient of a Discovery Award from 92NY's Unterberg Poetry Center, a Pushcart Prize, and fellowships from the Kenyon Review Writers Workshop, Idyllwild Arts, and Poetry at Round Top. Mag's work can also be found in *The American Poetry Review, The Paris Review Daily, Copper Nickel, Poetry Daily,* and elsewhere. Mag has an MFA from UC Riverside and a PhD from Texas Tech. She lives in Dallas, Texas and teaches at Southern Methodist University.

www.ingramcontent.com/pod-product-compliance
Lightning Source LLC
Chambersburg PA
CBHW030534080526
44586CB00011B/434